Pr̶

for Andriette

GW01460219

"Andriette is in a class by herself. ᴗᴎᴄ ᴦᴀᴅɪates the very message she shares. Andriette lights up the room with her presence and is a precious gift to the world."

—Rev. Terry Cole-Whittaker, author of the best-selling,
How to Have More in a Have-Not World and
Every Saint has a Past, Every Sinner a Future

"Andriette Earl-Bozeman has the eyes that look into the soul and sees clearly what needs to be removed for one to experience his or her original wholeness. She has a voice that speaks to the soul. When Andriette speaks, you know that you are connected to your own higher soul, your authentic self. It is clear that Andriette is inspired from a world beyond ours and has the keys to unlock the treasures within."

—Brother Ishmael Tetteh, an African Mystic and
author of *Soul Processing*

"I have had the special pleasure of designing and presenting a workshop with Andriette. I was very impressed with her clarity, integrity, and sense of humor, as well as her dynamic presence as a speaker. She is a great teacher of how to use spiritual principles in every-day life."

—Carol Adrienne, Ph.D., author of
When Life Changes Or You Wish It Would and co-author of
The Celestine Prophesy: An Experiential Guide

"I'm convinced that Andriette's tremendous success during her career with Pacific Bell was a direct result of her ability to draw out qualities in others that they were not able to see in themselves. She was consistently recognized as a leading sales person and trainer and she effectively translated those skills into successful training programs for her company (Your Personal Success). Andriette has developed a unique style for helping people succeed in their career aspirations and resolving life issues by creatively applying universal life principles. This book is yet another illustration of her mastery. She is clearly one of the leading "Human Development Specialists" in our time."

—Rev. Ahman, author of
The Dynamics of the Spiritual Mind Treatment

"Andriette is a phenomenal woman! She is a Master teacher, trainer and spiritual guide who speaks her word with force and conviction. She inspires us to aspire to our very best selves. It is my honor to know her and love her."

—Rev. Elouise Oliver, Minister,
East Bay Church of Religious Science

EMBRACING WHOLENESS

LIVING IN SPIRITUAL CONGRUENCE

Andriette Earl-Bozeman

Edited by Jean Wiley

Cypress House

Fort Bragg, California

Embracing Wholeness: Living in Spiritual Congruence
Copyright © 2002 by Andriette Earl-Bozeman
Edited by Jean Wiley

All rights reserved. No portion of this book may be reproduced in whole or in part, by any means whatever, except for passages excerpted for purposes of review, without the prior written permission of the publisher. For information, or to order additional copies, please contact the publisher:

Cypress House
155 Cypress Street, Fort Bragg, California 95437
800-773-7782 / Fax: 707-964-7531
http:\\www.cypresshouse.com

LCCN 2002107080
ISBN 1879384515

GYE NYAME (*Except God*)
Ghanaian symbol of the omnipotence of God.
Abode santan yi firi tete: obi nte ase a onim n'ahyase, na obi ntena ase nkosi n'awie, Gye Nyame. (This Great Panorama of creation dates back to time immemorial, no one lives who saw its beginning, no one will live to see its end, except God.)

Cover design by Chuck Hathaway, Mendocino Graphics
Author Photograph by Allum Ross

Printed in Canada
2 4 6 8 9 7 5 3 1
First edition

Let the words of my mouth,
and the meditation of my heart,
be acceptable in thy sight,
O Lord, my strength, and my redeemer.

Psalm 19:14

DEDICATION

To my beloved mother, Estella Earl-Cook, "Nan", for the love, integrity, clarity and sense of personal power she resonates.

To Ada G. Jenkins, my amazing "Granny", a magnificent model of pure faith and trust.

To my precious godmother, Katie Parker, whose unconditional love and acceptance buoy me always.

To the ancestors, with whom these three women masterfully collaborated to shine their light so bright and aim it so high that I am completely surrounded and enfolded in their light, and could never, ever be truly lost.

I am enormously blessed as you continue to illumine my way and inspire my journey.

ACKNOWLEDGEMENTS

My heart overflows with gratitude and appreciation.

How absolutely magnificent it is to know that the power and presence of God surrounds and enfolds me wholly and completely. I give thanks that this entire project was blessed before we began and is forever more. I give thanks for the divine idea behind this work, for all those who contributed in the numerous roles required to bring this from vision through realization to form, and for all the powerful supportive relationships spawned throughout this magnificent journey. I give thanks for the straight ways, the twisting roads, the appearance of dead ends and detours, and a clear and steady vision of divine completion.

I give thanks and praise God for—

My beloved husband, teacher and friend, Darryl Bozeman, for his love, support and encouragement. I know I am all the brighter for basking in the light of his love.

My sisters, Winnie, Loreeta, Talibah and Valda, who remind me that we are the answer to our ancestors' prayers.

My literary midwives, Belvie Rooks and Jean Wiley, who doubled as angels providing love, inspiration, vision and guidance to ensure the timely birth of this book.

I would also like to thank Cynthia Frank, Stephanie Rosencrans, and John Fremont at Cypress House for their professionalism, willingness, encouragement and magic. Thanks also to Shiree Dyson and Marla Greenway for their willingness to stand at the ready through all phases of the manuscript.

Reverend Ahman and Anita Underwood for their generous contributions and steadfast belief in this project and me.

God has blessed me many times over with awesome life-supporting sister-friends, and I am grateful for their love, inspiration and wisdom: Suzzette C. Johnson, Mary Mitchell, Renee Threadgill, Sylvia Fortenberry, Susan L. Taylor, Morayo Imani and Ahmondra.

Reverend Elouise Oliver and my extended spiritual community at the East Bay Church of Religious Science.

For this and so much more, I am eternally grateful. I am truly blessed! And I give thanks.

ACHÉ

TABLE OF CONTENTS

INTRODUCTION

A TESTAMENT OF FREEDOM

*W*riting this book has been a lesson in love, letting go, trust and obedience. I had been "writing" this book for years and yet I had no book. There were numerous conversations and plenty of encouragement about me writing a book. No book.

The day I heard myself promise my dear friend, Susan, "I will have a book or at least a booklet by..." I knew I had set a powerful cause in motion. There was no turning back and I had no idea how to go forward and deliver on my promise. I cried. I immediately shared this with my sweetie pie, Darryl, and cried. Later that same day I was literally compelled to blurt it out to my friend, Belvie, and I cried. She said, "We can do this." With such certainty I believed her, I trusted and I cried.

I cried because I knew I would have to let go. I knew it would not be easy. I would have to let go of *something*. *Something* that had become so comfortable and familiar it roamed around within my mind as if it had joint tenancy in my belief system. Some time ago, I'd allowed *something* access to my fears and doubts and *something* began to influence and thereby limit who I was, how I was and what I could become. I had also acquiesced to *something*, agreeing to talk vividly about my vision instead of living it fully. I still had a lot of crying to do.

Indeed, I cried and trusted. Rather than renegotiate, I committed to keep my promise. In committing to my promise, I committed to my life. I knew *something* would have to die. It was so scary; I held my breath. I trusted. I had to remember and remind myself to breathe. I trusted. As I allowed myself to be breathed, I withdrew my breath from *something*. I trusted. I got stronger in my resolve to BE and *something* got weaker. I trusted. I was clear that *something* only had the power I gave it. All this time it worked off my power—*something* never had power over me! When I reclaimed my power, I found the strength to surrender, to let go. I prayed and asked others to pray for me, that I would stay out of my own way, that I would allow Spirit to have Its full sway, that I would trust and be obedient. I cried and I trusted.

When Belvie called Jean and she agreed to usher me through, I cried and I trusted. I cried and I trusted throughout the project. Jean revealed to me a book that wanted birthing that *something* had prevented me from seeing. I cried, I trusted and I was obedient—I was ready to see what else was there. I had experienced glimpses, the dribs and drabs, a few inspiring insights that *something* let get through. Now I was allowing it all to flow. Darryl, Susan, Belvie, Jean, Ahman and Anita led an informal support team of family and friends who prayed and encouraged me through. As a result, I knew more often than I doubted and I seldom heeded my doubts. I trusted and I obeyed. Providence moved, and I got out of its way.

Through it all, I cried. I prayed. I trusted. I obeyed. I surrendered. I allowed others to love and support me. I loved me and let *something* go.

Six months ago, with my knees knocking and almost stuttering, I affirmed freedom. Just like my promise to Susan, I set a powerful cause in motion. I offer this book as a testament of freedom. I let *something* go and *something* set me FREE!

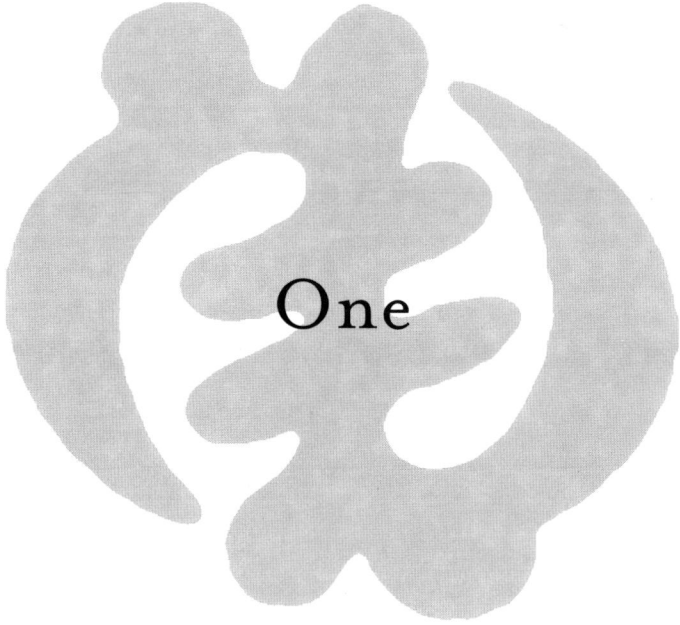

One

When Jesus saw him lying there, and knew that he already had been in that condition a long time, He said to him, "Wilt thou be made whole?"

John 5:6

EMBRACING YOUR WHOLENESS

Why Not Take All of Me

I am worthy of the bounty of good life offers me.
I declare it, I claim it, I accept it and I embrace it.
I am grateful God is good.

The Universe Awaits Your Order

*I*magine a "Universal Restaurant" where you, your friends and family go to receive your spiritual nourishment. This restaurant offers an extensive array of culinary experiences. Upon seating, diners are offered a huge menu-book containing sections with divider-tabs to organize the different "taste" preferences. Although the menu book is comprehensive, the restaurant also posts on a handwritten chalkboard a "favorites" list of the most frequently ordered meals. Most diners order from the chalkboard without consulting the full menu; many do not even bother to open it. Some guests are overwhelmed by its sheer size, while others don't want to take the time to explore. Some simply order the same dishes time after time, and miss the opportunity to select from among the larger presentation of delectable choices and thus expand their dining experience.

The restaurant staff realized years ago that 80% of the diners ordered from the first five pages of the menu book, and most of them stopped within the first three pages. Since the staff remained committed to offering a full array of choices, they continued to distribute the large menu and only reluctantly, as a convenience, set up the chalkboard of favorite and familiar dishes for those unwilling to explore more possibilities.

There are a few interesting things about the chalkboard. First, it contains only a fraction of the culinary delights offered in the menu book. Second, it contains none of the "light" meals the restaurant lists in the second half of the menu book. Thus most diners never know that the meals of love, joy, forgiveness, compassion, freedom, beauty and peace are available to them. Why Not? Because the chalkboard from which they choose to order lists only some of the frequently ordered dishes, the dishes that happen to appear in the first section of the menu book, the "heavy" section that offers servings of resentment, anger, attachment, resistance, regret, guilt, criticism, and shame. Thus 80% of the diners never turn to the "light."

How does that apply to your life? What possible choices and opportunities might you be missing because you select your experience from the meager offerings that others have chosen? It serves us to take an expanded look at all of the possibilities the universe offers us. Life is good and very good and provides all that we long for, all that we need. We are, responsible, however, for claiming it for ourselves. Sure, we may have to turn through several pages of lesser choices to get to what we *really* want. We have to believe and know that the good we desire already exists and is available to us. All the good you could possibly desire is awaiting your command.

So we may want to consider following the lead of the occasional diner at the "Universal Restaurant," the one who, after consulting the full menu, orders a dish that inspires awe among the other diners: "What's that? How did she know to order that? It's just what I wanted." Some assert that the staff should have told them how to order, should have told them of the opportunities they were missing. The Universal's staff members are trained to respond to these expressions of resentment with a quiet reminder that they are always poised to answer inquiries and respond affirmatively.

The Universe is asking: "Your order, please." So what would you *really* like?

It's Your Life — You Wrote the Script

As you place your order, remember that we cannot *shrink to greatness*; we cannot limit our opportunities while expecting fuller, richer lives. Nor should we be reluctant to ask for what we want. Our beliefs and words have tremendous power to limit or to enrich our lives. Essentially, it is all prayer—all of our beliefs, thoughts, and words bring forth a manifestation of what we believe and express. We create it all and we decide whether we are ordering a real delight or a challenge, or whether we're writing the script for a love story or a horror movie.

I am a living example of writing and starring in a horror movie under my own production and direction. I also insisted on doing my own stunts, and all special effects were at my expense. Like most horror movies, mine has powerful drama and gnashing of teeth—all the makings of a real blockbuster! There are scenes of an early marriage and divorce, a rape, two suicide attempts using pills, and even a scene that shows me placing a gun to my head. Yes, I have written many scenes of anguish, shame, betrayal, guilt, and regret. The plot builds until the camera finds me standing alone in the middle of the night on a freeway ramp high above the whizzing cars and trucks, and contemplating jumping.

Cut to the final scene. I am approaching the dreaded door. You know, the grotesque heavy metal or wooden or stone door that is always in the old horror movies. Well, there I am. And now the viewing audience gets involved. "No, no, run. Don't go through that door, girl!" Why does the audience shout to me to stop? They watched me create the path to the door, so, they know that a dreadful experience awaits me behind it.

How did the star end up out there on the freeway that night? How did she get even close to that dreaded door? Well, she carefully thought, believed, and then acted in accordance with her beliefs. There was a specific and unique combination of thoughts and beliefs required, and she had to repeatedly think and believe them in order to play this scene. And if she doesn't change them, well…

Cut to the special effects. Take our damsel in deep distress out of the frame and put yourself in her place. You now have the star role in your own self-produced, self-directed and self-financed horror movie. You are standing in front of the dreaded door; you can hear the sounds of chaos and smell the odor of fear and decay on the other side. Will you cross the threshold and enter further into this horror experience? As you pause before the door, remember this: Thinking X got you here, continuing to think X will keep you here. Only when you think something other than X will you create results different from X.

In his book, *Handle with Prayer*, Alan Cohen says that to think is to create. "The notion of something coming into existence without a thought preceding it is as preposterous as a flower growing without a seed to start it."

All thoughts create according to their own kind. Which are you choosing? An Oprah or a Jerry Springer viewing experience? Early morning meditation or TV news? The present or the past? The cause or the effect? Whatever is in your life was thought and declared there! And you attracted to yourself more of the same. You get to believe and experience whatever you want. Wholeness is a choice. So is brokenness. "Wilt thou be made whole?"

Are you willing to choose a different thought? What will it take for you to choose a different idea? It doesn't necessarily require an original thought, just a different one, an idea that will shift your focus to a different outcome, an outcome you want, not one you dread. It may be something as simple as a rhyme you've recited since kindergarten, or an affirmation, a hymn, a prayer. Your opportunity is to *be*—open and willing to accept all the goodness in life, knowing that it is all divinely decreed. So it must be GOOD!

The most significant difference between the way I was when I thought suicide and self-denial were the solution, and the way I am today is that now I know that the life I live is good and very good.

It's your life – you are writing and re-writing the script even now.

What If I Decided My Word...

What if I decided that my word *actually* meant something? Then I would probably be more conscious of how I am using my word. Wouldn't you? For example, "learning" is different from "doing." Am I going to *learn* to make better choices, or am I going to just go on and *make* better choices?

My sense is that the universe responds to the first like a crotchety old man, with a "Hhffmm! I thought you wanted to *do* something!" Learning is in the doing. Learning to play an instrument requires playing an instrument. Learning to be with another in a different way requires *being with*.

I envision the universe responding to our conscious and unconscious words, including those words voiced with the sole intent to impress others. What happens is an opening of possibilities, a universal process of setting a new course in action. It is the same process that is launched when a child tells his loving guardian that he wants to be an artist, a swimmer, or a veterinarian. The loving guardian responds almost immediately to encourage the child's new interest. To the budding artist, paint sets and drawing paper and crayons appear as if by magic. Aunts and uncles show up to take him off to museums and art galleries. He is given every opportunity to act as an artist.

So it is with the universe. When we say, we "want to learn x," we implore the universe to offer the appropriate lessons. But the lessons nearly always require the doing. We may long to learn to play the piano, but the learning comes in the playing. No amount of music books, no amount of time spent learning to read music, will have us playing the piano until we sit before it with our fingers moving along the keys. And if we are not judgmental about our progress, if we avoid self-mockery, we're soon playing—and sounding good, too!

Yes, we must be mindful of our words, because our words are born out of our thoughts and beliefs, and our actions are certain to reflect our beliefs. I will go on record with my guiding beliefs and the words I use to express them:

> I believe Love, Peace, Joy and an Abundance of all things good to be the goal of life and that this is attained the moment I believe.
>
> I believe that Truth is revealed in my life and through me as I live in close contact with the Indwelling Spirit.
>
> I believe that my word commands the Law.
>
> I believe I am Whole, Complete and Perfect.
>
> I believe my thought, word and deed design and direct my entire life experience.
>
> I believe that God is good ALL the time.
>
> I believe that I am Blessed.
>
> I believe that God is ALL there is.
>
> I believe that the life I live is God!

Embracing Wholeness

With beliefs such as these, I am definitely ordering differently from the "Universal Restaurant." I've also tossed that old script and I'm busy writing another one, again with me as the star. This time, I started from a longing and willingness to be whole. And for help and inspiration, I went straight to Scripture.

John 5:1-9 has Jesus at the healing pool of Bethesda. We are told there are a "great number" of disabled people lying around the immediate grounds. Jesus approached a man who had been lame for 38 years, and he asked him, "Wilt thou be made whole?" (Would you like to get well?)

"I cannot, sir," the sick man said, and went on to explain that he was unable to get in the pool, that he had no assistant to help him. Jesus told him, "Stand up, pick up your sleeping mat, and walk!" Instantly, the man was healed! He rolled up the mat and began walking!

Today though, I think maybe the brother might be better served by leaving his sleeping mat behind. (I'm sure this poolside community has a "bulk pick-up" service that will haul his mat away at no charge). Remember, the Scripture says he had been on his mat for some 38 years! I don't mean to offend anyone, I'm not trying to improve on or disagree with Jesus. However, I have some concerns about our brother leaving the pool with the same prop that supported this long-playing serial. Think of it: "Man by the pool can't get in the water or walk away. Tune in tomorrow when we hear our down-trodden brother tell us all about how he came to be in this deplorable condition and how much longer he will remain in this state." Can I just interrupt and say, "Leave the mat, my brother. *Please* leave the mat!" It has served as a central prop in this melodrama and now can only serve to connect you to this past—the very past you intend to exit." I cannot speak for the rest of you, but in my script, I leave the mat and exit stage right. It's doubtful that after 38 years I could sprint, but you would sure see me making haste to get up out of there, all the time shouting, "Thank you, Jesus!"

My remake of that horror movie I told you about? Let's call it "For The Whole Inner Child Who Has Considered Suicide, When the Rainbow is Way-More Than Enough." Yes, the rainbow is enough, the universe is enough. I am enough in my willingness to embrace wholeness and accept the beauty of my life.

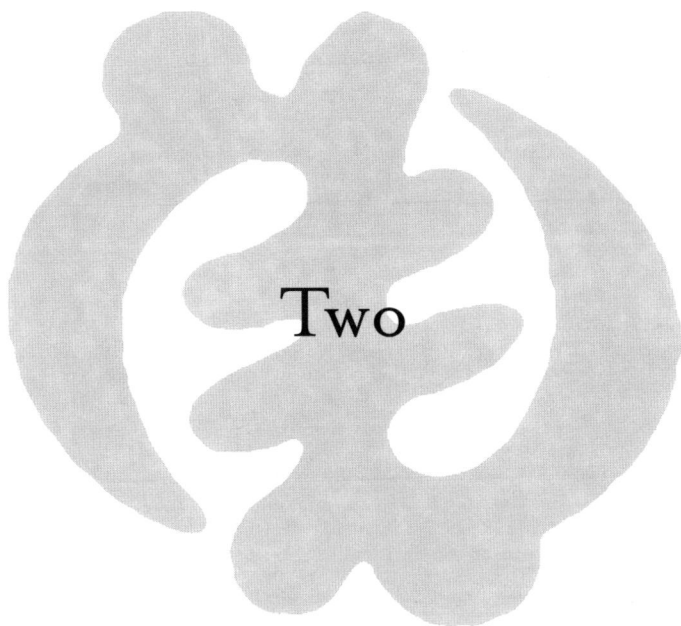

Two

Wisdom is the principal thing; therefore get wisdom:
and with all thy getting get understanding.

Proverbs 4:7

LEAN NOT ON YOUR OWN UNDERSTANDING

You've Got the Hook-Up

I surrender into the certainty of the Law of good.
My life overflows with good.
I see Universal goodness actively expressing as my life.
I focus on the good in my life and it multiplies.

*L*ean not on your own understanding. Don't continue hanging out where you are when you know that you don't want to be there anymore. Have faith that there is something that will transport you. Have faith that there's a transformation already happening within you that you can simply allow to evolve. Have faith that all the goodness of the universe is available to you right now. Be available and willing, open and believing. And for goodness sake, do not be deceived or restricted by your understanding.

The Bible advises us not to lean on our own understanding. Why? Because our human understanding is insufficient. If we lean on our own understanding, we are not only missing our hook-up to infinite possibility, but we are investing in it, relaxing in it, thinking it is supporting us when in fact it is too fragile and incapable of revealing the infinite possibilities awaiting us. The risk of leaning on our own understanding is that we can end up worse off than we already are—wounded, despairing and "making do." So let us not lean on our own understanding, at least not before we are clear about what it is we understand. And rather than invest time in getting clear about our current understanding, why not just have faith? Why not trust the universe? We get to choose. Let's just decide now. Are we going spend our time figuring out what we understand about our life as it is now, the same life that we're not even enjoying? Or are we going to expand our faith in a better tomorrow? Oh well, that settles that! I choose faith, and I release any temptation to delve into details that aren't satisfying me anyhow.

There Is a Power

The great philosopher Ernest Holmes wrote, "There is a power for good in the universe and you can use it." Well now. Yes, I knew there was a power for good. I saw folks actually using it; I saw it made manifest in their lives. Ah, but nobody had addressed me directly and told me that *I* could use it! I had managed to believe that perhaps some folks were born using it. Maybe some folks had a little secret hook-up. Maybe other folks had an "in." Maybe some folks knew somebody I didn't know. Perhaps some folks had a way out and I only knew the way in. But no, the words told me that I, too, can use this power for good.

A magnificent "power for good." It reminds me of an infomercial. I love infomercials and I don't mind admitting it, and I am sure I'm not the only one. Do they not convince us persuasively that we can use it—whatever the product happens to be? We may not even have hair, but show us a clever infomercial and we begin wondering if we couldn't just use that new hair product. We may not have known we had a problem, but a good infomercial will convince us that the new gadget being advertised will solve it, and we are soon writing down the 800 number. Sure, we think we may not need it right now, but maybe we can use it in the future. It slices, it dices. Oooh, we can use it! Those infomercials are powerful stuff. They sell! There is a power for good in the universe, but it is not about to advertise on television. It is there and available to each of us. Simply there. *Always* available.

Please do not lean on your own understanding! Because if you go with your own understanding, you may "understand" yourself out of believing in both the existence of good in your life and its immediate availability to you. Trust *this* infomercial: *You* can use it. You can use the universal power for good that is flowing within and throughout everything. You cannot get this wrong, because it is already set. The thing is, though, you cannot get there, to that place of using it consciously and intentionally, by leaning on your own understanding. There probably is no fertile place for this belief even to take root in your current understanding. That is the risk of leaning on your own understanding—you miss out, big time. You may even get a double dose of other things not very satisfying.

Pain for example. We think we understand what causes us pain— we just cannot figure out why it has to come our way so often. Relax. Breathe through it. Pain can make great fertilizer, and every farmer, every serious gardener knows the importance of fertilizer. It stinks, it's heavy, it requires hard labor—and yet the serious gardener is eager to work with it, mix it into the soil, knowing that somehow, it will work, *unseen*, to create the lovely garden she is anticipating. Just so, our painful experiences can enrich our lives; when used properly, they can set a new and positive course in our lives. That is, if we are not too busy hanging out in the pain, being actively engaged in suffering.

Pain is inevitable, but suffering is optional. There's going to be pain. So let us stop hoping for a life free of pain and start figuring out how to use the pain we encounter to enrich the soil of our lives. We do not have to suffer, though. We get to choose. We get to know that there is a huge universal process that we can trust to work in our good—despite how desolate things may appear to be. Let us lean not on our own understanding, but on the love of God and wisdom of truth. What may appear to us to be stark barrenness may transform our lives to a level of abundance we could not have imagined. I am consciously choosing to accept the pain, knowing that it is a consequence of life and living, of what I am asking for, what I am embracing, what I am accepting as the goodness of my life.

A Fertile Soil

Nature has a way of paralleling our lives and teaching us important lessons. I have read about the danger of soil depletion. It is a natural consequence to planting the same crop again and again and again. (As some of us continually behave to our detriment, doing the same thing over and over and over again—with diminishing results.) It may take years, but the soil starts to degenerate, and the land loses its lushness, its fertility. It is an excellent metaphor for our lives. Many of us keep right on planting the same crop in the same spot in the same way, again and again, leaning on our own understanding. And we wonder why we harvest the same crop, why we experience the same undesirable outcome in our lives. Blind repetition leads to depletion, even ruin. Surely that is not what we want.

What if we try faith? Suppose we trust that if we do things differently, there may be more flowers and soil rich enough to produce a lifetime of abundance. It doesn't have to be a drastic difference. We might merely think "maybe" instead of "no." We might try "could be," and then still ourselves. Really hush. Just experience the silence. Forget the rest that we may be tempted to say, that other part where we expose the fact that we're still leaning on our own understanding. How about "possibly," a simple word that creates the space for something else to take root.

Genesis offers us this fresh idea: "In the beginning, God." This is the source of my core belief: God is ALL there is—there is nothing else. "In the beginning, God." Now, that is enough to keep us busy, fully engaged and challenged. It is enough to have us confront old beliefs and renew our minds—and transform our lives. "In the beginning, God" says to me that any question I might pose around whether so and so is God also or how such and such circumstance in my life can be an expression of God—any such question must be responded to affirmatively given that, "In the beginning, God." Even if we attempt to fast-forward to the "end" in my book of life , we still find GOD. There is no-thing else. No matter how I twist it, turn it, examine it, try it, test it, deny it... God truly is *All* there is.

When I hold a sunflower seed in my hand, I am blessed and absolutely awed by the realization that within it is the substance from which a truly beautiful sunflower can grow. Last year I planted sunflower seeds for the first time, and I watched as they grew into the most beautiful giant sunflowers—towering thick stalks and huge yellow blooms containing hundreds of seeds like the ones I had planted. It is in awesome wonder and certainty that I look within the puny, weird-shaped sunflower seed to see that it contains within not only a magnificent, imposing bloom but also a new generation of seeds that will ensure eternal life for this flower species. That seed is faith at work, God at work.

If we have faith that in the beginning, God, then we could choose to be silent and still and simply allow the rest of the story of our lives to be revealed through this belief. For all eternity, God. What if we trust that *maybe* that really is all there is? Then we might have a sense that not only are we already living in infinite possibility, but we are already who we are becoming. Now, we may not be manifesting that divine possibility at present, but just because we are not manifesting it does not mean it is not the truth about us. Not manifested, yet? Do not let the facts distract you from truth.

Cosmic Hook-Up

My experience with my new computer provides a perfect example. My loving husband heard my plea and bought me a new computer as a birthday gift. He got the works: state-of the-art computer, large monitor, faster modem—and the services of a computer technician to hook everything up and install all kinds of programs. I tell you, I am hooked up! I have yet to discover what all I have in there. Every now and then I may call the technician to tell him something else I think I might need for him to install. Invariably he tells me I already have it, that he's already installed it. Well, okay, but where? Sure enough, when he walks me through the process, there it is on the screen, staring me in the face. The fact is, I never used it because I did not know it was there; and the truth is, I had it all the time. The solution, the software, was there whether I knew it or used it. It was always there for me.

Thankfully, I do not have any belief that I am more loved by the computer technician than I am blessed by God! So I do not have any belief that the brother, as baaad as he is, hooked me up beyond the way God did in the beginning. In order to engage the universal power for good, we have to have a sense that it is there. If I'd continued to lean on my own understanding, I would still be typing in some antiquated word processing program. And so I live my life, leaning on my faith, not on my limited—and very human—understanding. And I am aware that I can circumvent my faith by doubting. Some of us use doubt to neglect our good. It's all there for us—the latest version, all hooked up—and yet off we go, acting as if to prove it's not there, digging up versions of an old story typed on antiquated software.

Have faith in the good of the universe. Know first that life only does for us what it can do through us. Have faith that you are the artist painting your canvas, you are the writer writing your story, and that you will only paint and write what you are *willing* to see, to experience. You have short-circuited your artistic gifts when you lean *only* on your understanding.

Hanging Out with Joy

It is said that joy comes in the morning. Now I know that's true, and the reason I know it's true is because I have not always been willing to see it. You see, I've crawled under the bed at night, with whatever fear and drama I had going on, trying to hang on till morning. Much like the guy in the film, "Groundhog Day," who was unwilling to call joy into his life and conscious awareness. He languished in cinematic "hell," reliving the worst day of his life over and over and over again. It took him several days to shift his attitude, expand his consciousness, and align his behavior with the joy that awaited him every morning. No, just hangin' on 'til morning won't get it. We have to know that joy comes in the morning.

Someone might argue that she looked for joy and it didn't come, but under closer inquiry she will reveal that she stayed deep under the bed all day. How can she be certain there was no joy for her in the morning? She was not at all amenable or available to joy. The truth is, we have to both *be* and bring the joy we desire. It's similar to a potluck brunch. If you really have a hankering for potato salad without egg, you'd better prepare it and bring it yourself. Want spicy tofu? Then make some and bring it! That is the essence of living in spiritual congruence: to have faith that joy *is*, then be it, exhibit it, and take some along to share it. Have faith that joy indeed comes as soon the sun rises in your life, as soon as you allow yourself to rise to a new understanding—the "morning" of your life.

That is why faith is so important. You do not crawl from under the bed to meet joy unless you believe that joy is out there. So that is why joy is coming for *some* of us in the morning: It comes for the ones who are there to greet it. It is not going to wake us with a nudge and a shake. We have to meet it in the hallway. Meet it down the street. But meet it always with enthusiasm and with anticipation.

We have to meet it with the kind of anticipation we feel when a beloved friend or relative comes to visit. We're so eager to see them that we're at the airport *early*. I have been at the airport to meet some folks when I wasn't even clear what flight they were on! We'll risk the traffic and the airport congestion to get there early. The airport's only so big, we think, maybe we'll just canvas it, maybe we'll take a friend to stay with the car. Have we not done that? And yet we *wait* for joy to wake us up. Joy comes in the morning for those who go out to greet it.

So go ahead, greet it, hang out in it and stay focused on it. This is important because sometimes we find ourselves on the brink of doubt. We begin to use our universal power for good, we see it working wonders in our lives—and then at first sight of the first apparent obstacle, we revert to our old limited understanding. Pretty soon, we have constructed a theatrical set and called in Central Casting to bring in some support characters: lawyers, accountants, witnesses—none of whom appeared in the original script. We have affirmed and prayed and meditated on our perfect outcome in this or that endeavor, and we are solid in our trust, we think. And then as soon as a challenge appears, we begin to doubt, to fear, to create tension and drama. Well, maybe there is good even in that challenge, maybe it is there to remind us to stay focused on *our own good*.

Hang In There

What to do? Stop leaning on our own understanding of what this challenge is about. Reach for a higher understanding and faith that our good is already showing up. Be still. And do not, *please* do not call Central Casting or build a case. Instead, in the stillness, know that you've got the hook-up to all the good you can handle. Know that it works all the time, everywhere, continuously. The challenge is knowing how to use it consciously and intentionally, boldly and courageously. Speak only the words you want to have manifest, and then speak them like you mean it!

In John 6:60, the disciples are telling Jesus that his message is a bit hard to hear, much less live by. "Master, this is a hard teaching." They explain that they understand why folks don't want to hear this teaching, because, once they gain clarity, they find that there's no one to blame for their affairs.

In other words, in our modern lives, we realize with clarity that the state of our affairs has nothing to do with the IRS or the utility company or the stock market. It has absolutely nothing to do with our ethnic group, culture, religious practice—none of that. It has everything to do, however, with the one looking back at us in the mirror.

As I remember the story, Jesus was cool, and said something like, "And does that offend you? Does that make you suffer?" For at no point had Jesus ever told his disciples that their road would be easy. He did not promise to take the low road, the easy path. Now they're complaining that it's a hard teaching. And I imagine Jesus saying, "I thought you knew, you've got to bring some to get some."

Does it make us fearful, does it make us suffer to learn that we are going to have to be conscious and intentional, that we will no longer be able to lean on our own understanding? Does it frighten us to know that we're going to have to walk in faith, even when our "dis-ease" makes us want to turn tail and run? Indeed it is a hard teaching. "Yes," I imagine Jesus saying to his homeboys, "but I know you are all up to it."

Well, I *am* up to it, and I know I am not alone. I am already on the journey, and admittedly, it is a tough road to walk sometimes. Yet how else am I going to plant my good if I don't hoe first? I have some seeds to plant, lots of prosperity ideas. I planted some visions a while back, and I am anticipating a magnificent harvest. "In the beginning, God." I know it is a hard teaching. But it is a good life, it is worth it. How to use this power for good? Use it, the best you can. Take the first step. And lean not on your understanding, but on a power greater than any circumstance in your life. How to use it? Believe that joy comes in the morning and then go greet it. Get dressed for it. Joy requires a wardrobe; so does prosperity. So if you're expecting prosperity in your life, then act like it, look like it, sound like it. Be congruent. Use all the tools: prayer, meditation, affirmation, and stillness. And find a prayer partner, someone who will remind you that you seem to be leaning on your own understanding in this situation, that you might want to lean on God, instead. Remember that joy comes whenever it is welcomed. Remember that the goodness of God is available to you at all times, in all places, under all circumstances, waiting to get your attention. So pay attention. Get out of your own way, and stop interfering with the divine process. There is a magnificent power for good in the universe. Use it!

Three

And God said to Moses, I AM WHO I AM and WHAT I AM, and I WILL BE WHAT I WILL BE...

Exodus 3:14

The Universe Says Yes to You—Always

Just Like Jell-O

All things are possible. I am open and willing.
I know the truth about who I am.
All the good I desire awaits my command,
so I declare divine goodness in every aspect of my life.

*T*he metaphor of cooking often comes to me when I reflect on God. No, I'm not a good cook, not even close. But I've known master cooks, grown up with them, delighted at sharing their memorable meals. You've probably noticed that there are those in the mastery of food preparation who, after they've put it all together in a most exquisite and delicious way, then make a little gesture with their hands, like slap-slap. An indication that they're finished, and now it's on you. The platters and serving bowls are overflowing, the food is hot and beckoning, the table's all set. So the rest is up to you. They're not at all concerned about how you use the sauce, though they began preparing it the previous night. They're not at all concerned whether you really put it on the dish it was intended for. They simply have prepared it and let go of it in its entirety, with satisfaction. It is absolutely up to you to enjoy it however you see fit.

And then there are the other master cooks who, having prepared an equally wonderful spread, as delicious and as exquisite, are very specific about how you should go about enjoying it: "Sweetie that isn't what I intended that to go with. That bread was to be saved for this other little thing that's happening here and the sauce should go on your vegetable, not over your rice." It's clear that they have a very specific idea of exactly how the meal should be enjoyed and they want to make sure you understand.

Well, I have a sense that in Genesis, when God hooked it all up and said, "This is good and very good," God then did a similar slap-slap of hands and said "I'm done." In my humanness I know that when I'm done with something and pleased with it, having hooked it up I'm *through*. I have a sense that anyone who is waiting for God to start tweaking Her work some more, adding a bit of this and that... Then, the wait is on. The truth is that the work has been done, and it is good and very good. I absolutely believe and am grounded in a knowingness that this is what God is doing in Genesis: on the one hand pleased with the perfection and magnificence of Her creation, and on the other hand, finished with it. The rest is up to us. My belief is that there is nothing new to be discovered, every "new" invention is using the stuff that's already here; every "discovery" is stumbling upon something that was already there. Check out Columbus' discovery.

There's a joke about a time when the scientists are going one-on-one with God. (We all do this anthropomorphic thing of giving God human qualities sometimes, and I like to do it because it helps to illustrate the point. We can see it and therefore we have a point of reference.) So, these scientists were having a one-on-one with God, attempting to challenge Her with their brilliance, asserting among themselves they were quite capable of doing what She's done, declaring among themselves that they had the scientific wherewithal and the knowledge base that She possessed. God is playing along, and at some point, She invites them to just do it, create something. "Let's get it on." As the scientists reach down to get some dirt to get started, God says, "Get your own dirt!"

Here's the bottom line: Everything we are getting ready to use, to create, to invent, to make manifest is already here as unformed substance. It is also called faith. We are simply reusing it, mixing it up differently, kneading it in a different way—but it's all there for us. That is the nature of God's completeness. So, whatever the life form, whatever the energy levels, God's work is complete. What does that mean for you and me? The breath of God is there for us, available to use as we choose, providing us with everything we need to live successful lives. It means we all possess awesome power. All that is required to use it is to connect with it, to bring it into our conscious awareness. The quality of our lives is in our hands, according to our vision. This is in fact the essence of the entire teaching of the New Testament: that God is all there is and that everything else in our lives is the human manifestation according to our willingness to use it, to sample the feast set before us.

We tend to allow our human experience to define the nature of God, rather than letting the nature of God define or inform our human experience. It means that in our human experience, when we are stuck on something or facing some challenge—in relationship or in our financial affairs for example—we may be defining the nature of God as something having to do with this or that particular mess in our lives. Instead, we should begin with an awareness of the perfect, divine and complete nature of God, and then we will see that this other stuff isn't even real, it can't be. It looks real, it even feels real, but it's a temporary condition that I can change, knowing that what *is* real, the real me, the divine me, has everything I need to fashion a better life.

To do otherwise would be like staring at your reflection in one of those fun house mirrors at a carnival. The mirror distorts your image, sometimes in grotesque ways. But it's not really you, it's just a reflection. Most of us have the consciousness in the moment that it's not the real us staring back. As children however, we thought some of that stuff we saw reflected was real—and that was scary. We have an opportunity to stop defining the divine based on our human experience. Let's start, right now, setting things straight.

Within everything that lives, there is One Life, One Energy and It energizes everything. All expression is formed from One Spirit. It is this mystical understanding that is revealed in Acts 17:28: "For in Him we live and move and have our being..." Our being is derived from the Allness, the divinity, the perfection, the wholeness, the completeness that is God/Spirit. It is out of that, that I have my breath. It is out of that that I have an idea of who I am. It is out of that, that I have an idea of what I am and how I am. It is out of that, *that* I am. There could be nothing else. Genesis spells it out beautifully. Anything else, we simply made up. It's not true! Like the reflected image in the fun house, it's not real.

As we stop looking at who we are and how we are from a very human perspective, and start embracing our lives from a divine perspective we understand that there has to be as much God right here as there is anywhere else. We also understand that there's as much God on the stormy coast of Maine as there is in sunny California, as much God in the Special Olympics as there is in the regular Olympics. Because it's all God. And if I'm seeing it differently, then I need to adjust my vision. I need to turn the *light* up a bit because I'm missing something that I know is there. It is the nature of God to be everywhere and always present. It's also the nature of God to give from Itself, to Itself, through Itself.

So let us return to the master chef, to the feast before us. The master chef says, "hook it up however you please, baby, however it would taste good to you." Inevitably there's someone who fills her plate then eats one thing at a time—perhaps first the bread, then the rice, then the vegetables, then the salad and last the fish. And that's all right. It is her individualized expression of the enjoyment. It is knowing that it's all God and it's all Good, however one chooses perfect manifestation. And that's exactly what this is about: perfect manifestation. There is a Persian aphorism that states, "The eye through which you see God is the same eye through which God sees you." We want to be careful so that we avoid manifesting our experience of God in our lives, by placing limitations on the possibilities that God places before us.

The Best I Can

Recently, I was honored to lead a meditation workshop in another city. As it happened, I gained important insight into stamina and courage. Now, I've set a goal for my physical health and I have been working out with a trainer. Together, we've been ratcheting up my level, and now I'm on spinning. Spinning is the process of working out on a stationery bike and building up enough momentum so that the bike spins the biker, essentially. (In that sense, it's a lot like prayer work. There is a point at which you're prayed up, a point at which you are simply riding the wave.) So there I am, spinning away, when I glance down and realize that my shoelace has come loose and is now entangled in the pedal. Oh no. I can see the way this is going to end, because my momentum is up and there's nothing in the moment that I can think to do. As I tried to tear my shoe off, I twisted my foot at such an angle that I injured both ankle and foot. Well, we did the ice thing but by afternoon I was in tremendous pain and limping badly.

Now you know I had a moment of doubt about going forward with that workshop. Maybe I should call it off, maybe I should try to reschedule. And then I thought to myself, look, I'm blessed to have work I absolutely love and am called to do. I'm doing this. I'm taking dominion. During the two-hour drive I had an icepack tied over my foot, with rubber bands. That helped some, but when I arrived I faced another moment of doubt. For I had been committed to offering a moving meditation as part of my presentation. The seated meditation part went fine, but now, with my ankle…I considered dropping the movement portion. The problem, however, was that at no point could I hear an internal "yes" around that as an option. And so I heard myself saying aloud, "I'll just do the best I can."

Let's freeze-frame that. Because I need to confess that I had no idea what "my best" was that day. In the human experience we seldom know what the best is that we can do. There are many who would challenge me on that. Some who might be inclined to say they tested something just last week and know exactly the best that they can do regarding X. My response would be, that's the best you could do then, but what about now? For instance, if you ran 10 blocks—the most you'd ever run and the best you believed you could do—I 'd have to suggest that maybe this week you could run 10 blocks and 6 inches or 11 blocks or possibly 20 blocks. I have a sense that we do not know the best we can do, and yet as we affirm it, it becomes a grabbling hook that either expands or limits our best in terms of future possibilities.

But back to the meditation workshop. I decided that I would just do the best that I could do—thinking of course that I'd limit the exercise, take it slow... and then see. The result of that initial, hesitant effort was that I did the entire moving meditation with the group and I didn't feel much pain! At first I was timid. And then I thought well, what's the worst that could happen. (I am sure you've been there, in that sense of "Well, I'm out here anyhow.") And I did a little more, and a little more, and by the time we finished there was no pain and no swelling. My best was a lot better than I thought.

Now this example really isn't just about me; it's also about you. You're not subject to a different set of rules, guidelines, laws or principles. What I've just described is an example of what is happening everywhere, always, because it's all God. The nature of God is that everything you need is all there for you, and that there's enough of it for infinite and eternal expression—whether it's getting through a movement workshop or fulfilling your highest dreams.

Jesus summed all of this up for us when He said, "It is done unto us, as we believe." Now I know that many of us don't want to hear that; we aren't quite sure we believe it. And yet we can judge by the results. If anger, messiness, or drama are showing up in our life experience, then there must be a belief system that is holding them there, even attracting them. I believe that we often suffer not because suffering is imposed upon us but because we have rejected our true nature, our connectedness to the divine Source. We do not have to suffer, though some of us may be choosing it over other options. I could have stayed home with my twisted ankle and had a completely different experience. I could have cancelled the workshop and suffered some more. And it would be fine. Problem is, I would never have known what I missed. Which is that my best is always getting better. The only way we know is to put it to the test. What a valuable lesson!

Casting My Mold

Maybe God is like Jell-O. Okay, okay. I know that some of us don't necessarily want to hear that you're playing around in Jell-O. But I believe God is like Jell-O to the extent that the minute you put a mold to it, you get what you set up. Are you with me? First there is that little box of powder you buy off the shelf. You mix it with water, put it in a mold of your choosing, refrigerate it, and voila! you have something. But *what* do you have? You have exactly what you decided. You have it now manifest according to the way you set it up. So it is with the nature of God. We have the experience of God according to how we set it up, according to the mold we chose to use. All we are doing is saying, Okay, God here's the mold I'm offering. I get to decide and today I'm going to be the one everybody picks on. I'm going to be the one that gets passed over. I'm going to be the one who gets laid off, or I'm going to be a nervous wreck cuz they haven't gotten to me yet but I know they're coming. That's the mold.

Now, someone else may be setting in place another mold that says, "it doesn't matter where I go, I'm all right. I'm all right here. If I leave here I'll be all right in the next job. I was all right before I got here. This mold says I'm all right and it doesn't matter where you set it, or what color you make it. Praise God." It is in fact done unto us as we believe.

On her CD, *In The Land of I Am*, Ricki Byars sings, "In The Land of I Am, I am more than I have been, I am more than I will be, I am all that I am." How will you be more unless you give more a chance? You know for sure you're more than you have been, because that's what got you here. You know for sure that you're more than you will be, because you're co-creating what you will be and you know as the co-creator it's got to be greater than the created. So whatever it is that you're commanding into being now, know that it's done from a place of tremendous power. Going in with a limp doesn't mean you can't come out running. Going in with a lisp doesn't mean you can't come out a great orator. Going in feeling like you're not all that doesn't mean you can't come out as all that—and more. We've simply got to shift our consciousness to more.

A major part of the shift in consciousness is to know the true nature of God and to know that it includes us; to know that we are the nature of God made manifest. The shift in consciousness means you get to decide which mold you're going to use. But we have to be careful. Recently someone was sharing with me a high intent of his. I was listening but I was also noticing his frown. I had to tell him to wipe that frown off his face, and fast. Because the frown was about to cancel out his high intent, his goal and his dream. His frown was about to take him straight to a place of resistance and doubt. We have an opportunity to embrace the larger context, to live our lives knowing that God is far more than we can imagine and far more generous than we may think we deserve. We cannot recognize this while we are believing that it's not. This idea is worth repeating: "We cannot recognize what is, while believing that it is not."

Reverend Ike used to deliver whole sermons around the theme,

"Get your 'but' out of the way!" In my practice I very often am talking to people who say they want such and such—but. "I know I have such and such on the ball, but... I know that I am desirous of a relationship and there's someone who cares deeply about me, but... I know that I want financial prosperity and I've started to save, but..." Reverend Ike is simply warning us that that simple word 'but' can wipe out everything we uttered before it.

That's the meaning in Hebrew 4 and 6, where it says, "They entered not in because of unbelief." We don't have the experience because we don't believe it's due us. We don't believe that the nature of God, in all of Its majesty and divinity, includes us: that we are the rightful heirs to the kingdom, the right ones to experience all that God is.

Too often our consciousness is that of a house divided against itself. We're wanting and declaring something wonderful, and all the while supplying the reasons why it can't possibly happen for us. "I'll never have that kind of partner because... I want that, but you see I... and they wouldn't." We're a house divided against itself. "I wouldn't know what to do with that much money." Is that so? Well guess what? You won't even have to worry about that, because you've set in place a mold that doesn't include that much money. If that is your mold, then it is already overflowing with some other stuff you just may want to toss—that you need to toss.

It's true that joy will come in the morning, but whether you get some or not will be up to you. You get to decide whether what you bring to be filled with joy is a thimble, a cup or a bucket. Joy will come in the morning, but how much will you get? That's why the example of George Washington Carver is so important— it wasn't that he had a license on the peanut. What he had instead was a willingness. He was the one who set his sights and was willing to say, " There's something more to this." And all the while you know somebody was waiting for him to let go of that peanut so they could eat it! Because somebody else was holding a different vision of what it was; a different vision of its possibilities.

So right here and right now there's an opportunity for you to stop focusing on how things used to be, and choose another mold, make another selection or create your own. Commit to taking dominion. It's true that your life is in God's hands. It's also true that my life is in God's hands. However, our different lives manifest differently according to the mold that we've set and it's in that sense that we are co-creators with God. I've thrown away the mold that says I'm not the one. I've thrown away the mold that says I'm too short, I'm too old, that says I'm too young. I've thrown away the mold that says I'm too generous, or not generous enough. I've tossed out all the molds that would diminish me in any way. In the Unity Prayer of Faith, I recite, "All things I am, can do and be through Christ the Truth that is with me." When we know it and say it with conviction the Universe always answers, "YES."

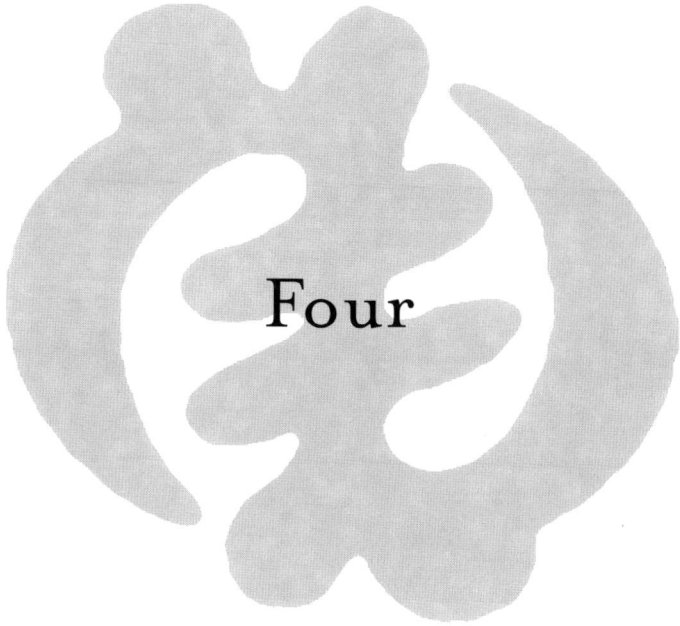

Four

And whenever you stand praying,
if you have anything against anyone,
forgive him...

Mark 11:25

Your Moment of Truth

Set Yourself Free

I surrender my will to LOVE and compassion.
I rejoice in knowing that all circumstances and
opportunities in my life are working together for good.
I remember and I forgive. I live in Grace.

I was blessed to have a spiritually cinematic moment at a local hospital, of all places. I was there because I had very severe flu symptoms. After consulting a doctor, I went to the hospital pharmacy to wait for my prescription to be filled. The pharmacy had one of those digital "ticker-tape" machines that I began to read half-heartedly. Suddenly a statement appeared that was so obviously intended for me, it made me wonder if anyone else could see, let alone read, what I was reading. It felt like a scene from "Field of Dreams" in which only Kevin Costner and the viewing audience could hear "The Voice." What came across was this: *Resentment is the same as ingesting poison intentionally and then waiting for the other person to die!*

I was thunderstruck and I quickly looked around to see if anyone noticed the profound impact that the statement had had. When no one else seemed to be particularly attentive, I wondered if I'd grown delirious.

Maybe it was the fever; maybe it was extreme fatigue—I don't know. I just know those words seemed to speak directly to me. How long had I held and harbored resentment? It had actually been quite a while.

I recall as a youngster, telling some persona non grata: "You'll be sorry— you'll see!"

Too often this was a warning that I was going to harm myself, unintentionally of course, in order to teach someone else a "well-deserved" lesson. Unfortunately I carried this pattern into adulthood.

Can you imagine anyone ingesting poison for the sole purpose of teaching another person a lesson? Well trust me it happens. It happens in many suicides, and many attempted suicides—sometimes there is a conscious intent to punish others. This same kind of resentment also shows up in self-destructive habits and addictions. The smoker, the over-eater, the alcoholic, the drug abuser is commonly a person who perceives herself as an undeserving victim, and strikes out—at herself.

I know of someone whose resentment to a nightmarish and violent attack festered so deeply that she actually sought out a "hit man" to find and kill her attacker. She thought that would put an end to her pain and rage. Of course that was just another way of ingesting the poison of resentment. Fortunately, Spirit guided her to share her search only with people who loved her, or that plan might well have been the beginning of true self-destruction. Ingesting poison and waiting for someone else to die? Unfortunately we do it all the time! Anytime we resent another and allow that resentment to fester, we are indeed poisoning ourselves with toxicity. The act of forgiveness is always more for us than for our perceived culprit. Forgiveness leads us to compassion, which leads us to love, which leads us back home to the love of God.

Forgiveness Leads to Compassion

By now, all of us know about the essential relationship of forgiveness to overall well-being, especially the relationship to excellent health. There are literally hundreds of books and audiotapes on the subject, and even research and academic institutions are beginning to study the healing power of forgiveness. There are, of course, variations on the theme, and now I am about to add my own because, I have found that some of us have problems with both the concept of forgiveness, and especially with the being and *doing* of forgiving. Well, first of all forgiving requires that we release all of the resentment, the anger and the fear that we have toward the people and circumstances that may have wounded us. Not everybody wants to release all that stuff, yet. Some of us in fact have constructed whole identities around our anger and victimhood. Second, forgiveness requires us to include ourselves in the forgiving. Buried beneath this mound of resentment is often resentment of self. There is embarrassment and even shame at how we may have conducted ourselves in certain situations. Even though it seems strange, not everyone feels ready to do that basic forgiveness of self. Some folks insist that they've not done anything that requires them to forgive themselves. Interesting. Third, forgiveness requires compassion and vice-versa, and some of us are not sure how we feel about compassion. Just look around at all the suffering we choose to ignore. Often we are content to blame the victims themselves and simply walk away. The truth, though, is that forgiveness and compassion are vital signposts on the path back to experiencing wholeness and learning to live a spiritually congruent and fully integrated life.

Our resistance to compassion and forgiveness may be the reason that the Bible contains so many biblical stories and lessons on these subjects. There is one story of Jesus arriving by boat, landing, and seeing a great multitude of folks milling around. He was moved by great compassion for them and he said they were like sheep without a shepherd. We are told that, "he began to teach them many things." Jesus' actions indicate a personal responsibility and accountability for using what we have and what we know to help and guide others. Those who know and have a true understanding of the role of the shepherd are expected to act differently from those who have no conscious experience of the love and the guidance the shepherd offers. After all, if the people had known better, they would have done better. We all would! No, Jesus didn't resent or blame them for their current state of awareness. Instead, he began to teach, to expand their consciousness. He lit the way by being the way.

Compassion Leads to Grace

As Bill Withers suggests in "Grandma's Hands," the deeper our feeling of compassion, the higher our experience of love, love to the hundredth power! Bill Withers' "grandma" never believed he did anything "wrong." There was never anything for her to forgive. She knew there was nothing you could ever do to diminish your soul, your wholeness. "That baby (of any adult age) is *not* scarred for life." Like compassion, the more you have found forgiveness within, the more profound yet simple is your understanding of life. For in compassion you are both willing and accepting. This is probably the reason we have all heard many a grandmother say, "Well, bless her heart." They all seemed to know that nothing other than compassion was needed. In Grandma's hands: compassion. In Grandma's words: forgiveness. In Grandma's heart: pure grace.

It is the transformative power of forgiveness that we must embrace; it is compassion that we must embody as the bridge that transports us back to love. This means we stop seeing people as culprits and worse, but as victims of their own limited understanding and worthy of our compassion and our love. It takes a great deal of courage to make this shift in consciousness. In some respects, our ability to manifest genuine compassion is our moment of truth.

The Courage to Stand

What about our moments of truth? What about those moments when we are called upon to put all our cards on the table, to expose our hand so to speak—to expose what we really believe and embrace in our lives? Peter had such a moment. (I am not a biblical scholar by any means, though I love to glean fresh insights from ancient biblical stories.) In the Easter story recorded in Matthew, Jesus is arrested and taken to the place where he will be tried and sentenced. Peter remains outside while Jesus is tried.

After some time, a maid comes to the door and asks Peter if he isn't also among Jesus followers. Silence. Then Peter goes, "Uh uh. Not me." Now that's a moment of Truth isn't it? After all, Peter has been seen hanging with Jesus. A few minutes earlier Jesus was his boy, and Peter was like, "I'm down with you, man. I'd never betray you, no matter what." But now when the rubber meets the road, Peter is like, "Ummmmm...not me. I'm not the one. I hardly know the man." Peter is asked three times and three times he denies knowing Jesus! It was his moment of truth, his opportunity to affirm what he believed. In denying Jesus, he denied himself, his divine self.

During these times in my life, as the rubber meets the road and I have my pop quiz and as I am confronted with my own moments of truth, I understand Peter. I mean, I *really* understand him! Like you, I am often where Peter was: Can I stand for and live in alignment with what I say I believe? Can I live a spiritually congruent life, a life in which all aspects of me are in harmony?

I am aware that a lot of it is about sheer courage. The courage to stand in my own moment of truth. The courage to take the pop quiz and use the results to grow and thrive. I could cheat on the quiz, I could apply only half of what I am capable of—and probably get away with it, might even get complimented. But I would know the truth, and I would know that what I'd given was only half done. In the moment of truth, I have to ask myself, exactly what I am serving up. So I ask those who are willing to pray for me, to pray for courage. To pray that in my life, I show up. And I mean *really* show up. I don't mean get dressed and just appear, but show up fully; a prayer for courage that I wouldn't turn tail and do something less than what I'm called to be and do; a prayer that when called upon at the entrance, unlike Peter, I will say, "Oh yeah, I'm with him. I'm definitely with him. He belongs to me and I belong to him." Because I know it is the love of God that has brought me thus far. I know that I'm always riding the wave of that love. And I know that it behooves me to stand firmly in that belief and to declare it.

My prayer for you is that there would not be a moment when you deny your highest self.

I not only understand Peter, but I have great compassion for him. I understand faltering. I understand hesitation and habit and doubt. Throughout Jesus' ministry there were those who tried to undermine him, trying to make him prove himself again and again, insisting he perform yet another miracle. And the persistent threats of persecution and the hounding! Today he would probably be investigated and wiretapped. Peter had consistently hung in there with Jesus all the way. Remember, in Matthew 16:18, how Jesus confirmed Peter when he was the only disciple to recognize and declare Jesus as "Christ, the son of the living God." So Peter definitely knew the company he'd been keeping and yet, at a critical moment he faltered, he denied the truth, and in doing that, he also disclaims the truth about himself. He falters in his courage to honor and affirm truth. Playing this out over three times had to be devastating for Peter. In Matthew 26:75 Peter remembered what Jesus had said: "Before the cock crow, thou shalt deny me thrice. And he went out, and wept bitterly."

In the moment of truth what we reveal is what we really believe. What we reveal in that moment is how we have built the habits that form our lives. Because, what we do in those moments is largely out of habit—our habitual behavior. We all live habitually. That's an important admission and recognition. I have come to realize that much of what I do, I do simply because I've *been* doing it. The truth is, that is not reason enough. Habit is not intentional enough. It is comfortable and comforting, but it is not enough. Our habits expose our beliefs; they reveal the cause. It is like physics, the science of cause and effect. It is through my behavior that I reveal what I believe.

Stepping off the Cliff — The Bridge of Forgiveness

Belief requires your willingness to believe. When you believe it, that's when it happens. When you believe that it can be done, it will be done. There is a movie scene with Harrison Ford as Indiana Jones, where the bridge doesn't appear until he steps off the cliff. What do we need a bridge for if we aren't going anywhere that requires a bridge? Why would the bridge appear if we're not crossing the chasm? The one who does not believe there will be a bridge, should not bother trying to cross, since the bridge will not be there. But it will be for those who are trusting, determined, focused and willing to declare, "I'm out of here. It's time for me to go. I'm not even interested in what's coming and when it's coming. I am out of here now!" As they step out, the bridge appears. If we didn't know better, we might even think that it came out of nowhere. But because we know better, we know that it came from within.

Sometimes we construct beliefs rooted in error from the ton of facts we collect, then proceed to try and translate the facts into truth. There is no way to press down, roll up and present facts so that they then become truth. As we consider the moment of truth, know that the facts are largely irrelevant, and I praise God that they are. If not, then Peter could not have emerged from the facts that were staring him in the face. He would be stuck in depression, a self-deprecating paralysis. Peter somehow freed himself of guilt, blame, self-doubt and shame. Peter forgave himself, and in this forgiveness, he went on to do the work he was called to do.

There have been many times in my life when I have denied the truth about myself and I told someone in words and actions, "No,

I can't do it...I'm not enough and they'll never select me..." You know what? That's not true. That's not the truth about me. While I don't know whether I'll be selected, what I do know is that I come packing. I do know that I'm always bringing something. The something that I bring is my faith in the love of God. Pure love. It neutralizes all else. The perfection at the core of my being—and yours—never changed. You may not be doing that thing that you want to do and the way you want to do it, but that doesn't change the truth that you are perfect, that you are whole, that you are complete. You, too, are the love of God.

Getting Right Back Up

Sometimes we look to others and not to ourselves in our moment of truth. Often this is out of a need for sympathy and empathy, but also because we just want to see how far we can take the roles that we're playing. I am reminded of my youngest nephew, a toddler so full of divine energy and playfulness. What I've noticed is that when he falls or stumbles, he chooses one of three scenarios. In the first and most frequent scenario he picks himself up right away and continues his play, as though the tumble were part of it. In another scenario, he cries out in indignation and shows me the knee or arm he's just hurt. It is the third scenario that I find the most fascinating: the one where he looks at me and waits for my response to decide whether he's hurt or not.

Many of us have never outgrown the third scenario. We are still looking to the crowd to see if we're hurt and just how badly—and for how long. The crowd's response helps us to determine whether we are going to be down and out for a good while, or whether we should hop-up and keep going. During high school (bless my heart) I was a pompom girl. I recall an experience where I fell during one of our half-time routines. While stretched out on the gymnasium floor, I remember having the presence of mind to consider pretending as though I was really hurt. You know what I mean? Act as if I couldn't get up. I thought, if I'm hurt, or if the folks watching think I'm hurt then there's not as much shame as there is in just falling down. So I decided to just lie there and wait for the stretcher, wait for the concern and attention. After all, nobody laughs when they bring out the stretcher. As I'm on the floor trying to map out this scenario, I realize I'm about to get stepped on, that I am really about to get myself hurt. My co-pom pommers were busy with their dance and steps, and had no idea I had fallen. Pretty soon, somebody's foot was going to slam into my face. There was nothing to do but hop up and get right back in step.

Sometimes that's how life is. Rather than wait to find out just how badly hurt we are, or how many years of therapy this injury may require, or whether or not we're scarred for life or half of it, we might just want to get up and get right back into whatever we're committed to. We might just want to get busy being all that we can be. That might be our moment of truth. So you're down and out? What's the evidence? How many of us have pretended to be down and out? And then when we've finished with that act we get back up and we're just fine. Meanwhile the people who know us are wondering just why we felt the need to play that down and out role. Did we think that it became us? Was it something we really needed to experience?

Am I hurt? Well, maybe slightly and only on the surface. And as Grandma knew, "Baby, it's all gonna work out just fine."

So today I declare courage. I claim the courage, the trust and the faith of my grandmother and all my ancestors. For however they did it, they DID it! And just look at the magnificent wonders they co-created with God! Those wonders that are you and I.

Five

*For to everyone who has, more will be given,
and he will have abundance; but from him who does not have,
even what he has will be taken away.*

Matthew 25:29

ABUNDANCE IS YOURS
FOR THE BELIEVING
Living in Spiritual Congruence

I prepare my mind for prosperous thinking and living.
I plant only thoughts of good and this enriches my life.
I am open and receptive to infinite abundance.
All my needs are met and life is good.

*L*et's be clear about this: it's not about the money. The state of your financial affairs is a graphic reflection of the entire body of your affairs. So problems in your wallet and bank account are indications of problems in other aspects of your life as well—all blockage of the flow of plenty. If it's not flowing there, it's not flowing elsewhere—maybe not anywhere. Billie Holiday told us this in her classic song: "Them that's got shall get. Them that's not shall lose. So the Bible said, and it still is news." And she's right. Read it for yourself: Matt 25:29. This scripture explains how it is that "the rich get richer and the poor get poorer."

In order to manifest abundance in our life, abundance must first be in our consciousness. And we have to stay focused to get it and keep it there. Many people mistakenly consider money (and lack thereof) a totally different realm from spiritual development and wholeness. How many times have we heard someone say that her life is magnificent except for the money? How many times have we said it? It's time to put our attention where it belongs, and that usually requires a willingness to let go of a lot of beliefs about ourself and our money that are not serving us well, that are literally blocking the flow of prosperity into our life. The esteemed metaphysician, Catherine Ponder, offers this insight: That we are prosperous to the degree that we are experiencing peace, health, plenty in our world.

I am inviting you to take a moment to look at what is standing in the way of your prosperity, and financial freedom. What circumstance or person or belief are you allowing to block the flow of your prosperity?

Imagine that you are a crystal bowl, one that is overflowing with pristine water. When the bowl cannot hold any more water, the water continues to flow, spilling onto the table, the counter, and the floor. Note that it is only your size and shape that restricts the amount of water you can contain as the bowl. The universal flow keeps right on flowing, regardless. It just flows and flows. And you have access to it all. But first you must empty the bowl of all stones and debris, all the things that will limit your containment of this divine flow. As soon as you've recognized your distractions, let them go. Release them. Begin with an empty, expectant vessel available to hold all the good you can handle. For you see, your intent is to set a new course in motion, a new path that draws the flow of prosperity through you.

I truly believe that "the universe awaits your order." My sense is that in order to place your order, it helps to know what it is you want. When you order that piece of special furniture, have you not already declared that it is the piece you really want? By the time it's delivered, have you not already gotten rid of what used to be in that place? Remember, before the new piece of furniture arrived, you'd not only gotten rid of the old, but you have also dusted the floor, vacuumed the rug—prepared the perfect space for it. So let the old go, and replace it with something more appealing to you, something more compatible with your *intent* for that space and in this case, that space is your life.

Declaring Your Intent and Gratitude

In all of your affairs, and definitely in money matters, ask yourself what your intent is. Your intent is what you're willing to put your attention to, how you're willing to direct your energy. It's where you aim your light. So take the opportunity now to declare your intent concerning your finances. Be specific, and remember that intent is directly related to your values. It has to be. Any intent you declare that is not in alignment with your values is never going to happen. So take time to identify your highest values and match them to your intent.

For example, one of my highest values is contribution, which is why I do what I do. I don't know how *not* to do what I do, because I am so intensely guided to contribute to human development and empowerment. So I teach, I counsel, I offer workshops, I even deliver sermons sometimes. I don't think of myself as a public person; I'm actually quite reserved, even a bit shy. But I refuse to allow my reserve to interfere with my core value of contribution. I will not allow that.

Each of us has values that are so important to us that they actually define how we show up in the world. I'm encouraging you to take stock of your intent and explore your core values. And if they're not compatible with the intent you've set, if they're not in spiritual congruence, then you'll want to adjust one or both. You want to live a value-driven, a highly intentional life. We all do. Values and intent are parts of the engine that will jump-start the new experience you are creating: the flow of prosperity through you.

Here's a belief I have about financial prosperity: I believe that we have not because we "ask" not. And on those rare occasions when we have the courage to ask, we don't truly affirm it, we aren't surrendered to it. Sure, we say lots of stuff, we tell people lots of things about what we're going to do and who we are, and how we're changing. But we're not saying all this from our most authentic place of believing and knowing our power. And we're not willing to sacrifice, to give up the lesser for the greater. We're still holding on to the lesser because we're not willing to believe that there really is a pot of plenty. We're waiting for somebody to show us our specific pot before we affirm it—certainly before we're willing to give up the lesser we do see for the greater we do not yet see.

Well, here's the deal. You can't see your plenty through those eyes. Those eyes are focused on what you have or don't have right now. Your plenty is right where you are. Your eyes are looking over there. You will never see the prosperity overflowing the pot of plenty from where you've chosen to sit. Where we sit reveals our belief system concerning prosperity, our position in relation to our desired outcome.

Someone recently asked me about guilt: "What happens when you ask for money, and you get it, but you feel guilty?" Now can't you imagine the size of the stones in her bowl of plenty! There would have to be a substantial blockage for someone to experience guilt. What we want to feel is gratitude. When we begin to look at why we feel something other than what we want to feel, we should seize the opportunity to cut right to the chase. So, if I am declaring more money in my life and it arrives, what's my next step? To say, "Yes, thank you, thank you, thank you," out of genuine gratitude and delight. If I'm anyplace else, like stuck in guilt, I'm beginning to cut off the life source for that very manifestation of prosperity. Indeed, I might want to breathe in deeply, in such a way that my chest opens as if to indicate that I am open to receive even more. I'm saying to the universe, "If you think I loved that, watch me when you give me the rest of it!" When we receive the blessing in gratitude, we pass it on, and on. And because we are a part of that divine energy, it's always flowing our way. It is the nature of it. If plenty is not flowing our way, we are the ones stopping it.

Freeing the Flow of Good

Sometimes our confusion about what we call "income" blocks the flow of plenty. We tend to restrict it to wages and salaries. I prefer the term "incoming," which indicates so much more than a salary—a gift for instance—and creates a space for that wonderful sense of anticipation. So we're inviting the universe to bring on the plenty, to send it anyway it chooses. We're willing and ready to receive it, and we have numerous places it can come through. All kinds of places! All kind of opportunities!

There's another term I dislike, and for similar reasons: "fixed income." If you think your income is fixed, you are mistaken. Fixed means restricted. Well, the universe restricts nothing. You have been lied to. Worse, you've been believing it. There is "incoming." And if your incoming has stopped at a certain level, you have to go out and move the stones that stopped it, remove whatever fell into its path to stop it. No income is fixed—unless you're content with restricting it.

Do you agree that it isn't just about the money? Because in an overflowing, accepting, wide open consciousness there is no way that money can be the only good that isn't flowing. At issue here is the entire body of our affairs. At issue is our consciousness, our spiritual belief system. As we change our consciousness about money, we'll be setting a new cause to manifest an increased flow of prosperity in health, relationship, career—everything. For how you do anything is how you do everything. It's that simple.

Yes, we're focused on accepting and embracing Divine Spirit, Infinite Intelligence. No, I have absolutely no attachment to what we call It: God, Spirit, Absolute, Allah, Jehovah, Ja, It, He, She.... Call It whatever your prefer at any given moment. Just recognize and respond when It is trying to get your attention. And It will. "Look at me when I'm talking to you," as the adults used to say to us children. Maybe It's saying, "Give me your undivided attention as I am breathing you and living as you. Focus on Me."

The universe has an abundant supply, for you and for everyone. So there's something good and very good in the universe that's already ready and waiting for you. But some of us have proceeded to do things that keep us from the package of good that's sitting right on our doorstep, waiting for our attention. I don't know if we jump over it, or use the back door. We forget our knowingness, our being-ness, and end up missing the gift that is waiting for us. Is that what you are doing? Are you stepping over the good, crawling under it, unwilling to open it? Or are you letting it rot, so that by the time you get to it there may be no evidence that it was ever there?

"Put Some Away"

There is no amount of money that is so small that it can't be worked with successfully. Again, the keys are consciousness and intent. Remember, money is all around us, the evidence is there. Attracting money to your life is easier than maintaining a rewarding relationship, because money doesn't reject or confuse us—people do. So let us turn our attention to managing our money with intent. Ask yourself two questions: how much money does it take to live my life now? And how much money would it take to live my life as I want to live it? You need to know this. Let's say for example yours is a $20,000 life, but your incoming is $15,000. You are doing something that is out of integrity, because your incoming money needs to match or exceed your outgoing. What that means is that you need to live on less than your total incoming. Impossible? Absolutely not!

Consider the example of Oceola McCarty, who made her transition a few years ago. I met her when *Essence Magazine* honored her with an award. What an honor it was to meet her! She was an elderly African American woman from Mississippi who had been a washerwoman all her adult life. For years she was paid 25 cents, then one dollar a day. You may know the rest: Toward the end of her life, she donated $150,000 to the University of Mississippi. Now who among us is working for 25 cents? Who's working for a dollar a day? Whatever your incoming represents, we can safely assume it's more than hers was. And get this: Her $150,000 endowment was just sixty percent of her savings, not all of it. So when you start to believe that you can't live on less, please lift up the example of our Sister Oceola McCarty. She was an unassuming woman—with so much power, discipline and vision! She is such an excellent model for clear intent and aligned values.

Yes, I am always looking for models of people doing something that I aspire to, for all I need is an indication that it is possible. They don't have to pave the road, just step on the grass in such a way that I can see that somebody went that way, in the direction that I intend to go. Saving was in Miss McCarty's consciousness. It was instilled in her not to spend all her income. In an interview published shortly before her death, she said her grandmother had told her as a youngster, "Baby, put some away." And so she simply was obedient. And she put some away, and kept putting some away, for her entire life—in a savings account passbook. No CD or money market fund, no investment portfolio. She had had no formal education, but was Sister clear or what?! Her gift was to help African American students who might not otherwise have an opportunity to attend college. She would empower them; she would pave the way. Hers is truly the gift that keeps on giving.

A word about the appearance of saving and hoarding: They can look the same, but the intention and consciousness are *very* different. Hoarding comes from a consciousness of fear that the money flow will stop. Hoarding tends to indicate that there is no vision other than a dismal idea of what's happening right now. Saving, however, comes from a consciousness of anticipation and clear intent. Her neighbors may have mistaken Miss McCarty's simple lifestyle as hoarding her money. They may even have ridiculed her. Ah, but she knew the truth about her intent and went right on saving.

So, how much does it *really* take to live your life? And does it require that you spend beyond your incoming? Even as you are affirming and anticipating your incoming, you can practice saving now, today, however small the amount. There will be more. Just ensure that you always have something put away. It's all about developing your consciousness of plenty.

How much of your incoming is dedicated to debt? What percentage of it? The financial freedom you are seeking requires that you eliminate all consumer debt. All of it, every bit of it. The goal is to be debt-free. I am not including your mortgage. But cars are included—unless you're driving a limo as part of a chauffeur business you've established. If your car is not increasing your incoming, pay it off.

Try not to confuse debt with living expenses. Students have tuition and book expenses, but if you're no longer a student, that loan you took out is now debt, and it needs to be paid off. Your phone and energy bills are not debts, but monthly living expenses. Determine what percentage of your incoming can be selected for paying off debt. What percentage of your outgoing is going into your savings?

To be fully prepared, know that effective saving usually requires you to establish a spending plan, one that you will consult frequently to affirm that you are utilizing your incoming in alignment with what you intend, the goal you've set for yourself. However you choose to distribute your incoming, be certain that ten percent is going to savings, money to support you in manifesting the life you want to live, fully expect to live.

Add the spiritual law of tithing to your spending plan. There is no prosperity without giving back. It's a part of that whole universal flow. Tithing honors the practice of your intention, the higher vision you have of your life. You've heard the saying, "put your money where your mouth is." It's true that money does talk—

loudly sometimes, revealing what we believe and where we've placed our attention. Ten percent of the incoming is the standard, though we can begin with whatever we have, just to keep the idea in our consciousness. Many people give more than ten percent, out of gratitude and clarity about this principle.

Spending Consciously

Clear intent tempers the temptation you may feel to splurge, to stray too far from your spending plan. Let's face it: there is always a CD to hear, another movie to see, another must-have outfit. For many of us, there's always another pair of shoes. Trust me, I understand. After all, we live in a consumer society that teaches us the "joys" of instant gratification. Do your best to avoid the temptation. Ask yourself why you have to have it right now, especially since buying it puts you out of alignment with your intent. Learn to walk away.

Temptation is the reason that credit cards can be a trap for some. I suggest you that you use them like your checkbook—even better, your debit card. Now, that's presupposing that your checks clear like clockwork. Remember your intent is to be free of debt, so you pay off charges when the bill comes. You may use your plastic as you see fit, but ask yourself this: "Am I willing to pay this off when the bill comes? All of it?" And sometimes, right there at the cash register, you'll answer, no, no way. Try to stay conscious. We do too little conscious consuming. There will be a time for that other pair of shoes, perhaps with the very next inflow of money. Maybe you'll buy another piece of property—in good time, according to your intent and plan. Making a decision to live consciously and intentionally around our finances does not mean we have to miss out. It does mean we have to pay attention.

A budget seems to me to be a spending plan without the clear intent. It looks similar to a spending plan, but, again, the consciousness is different. For many people, a budget is similar to a diet—and just as distasteful and jinxed. Both diet and budget connote suffering. Rather than beat yourself up over not keeping a budget, simply begin to set up a plan for designing your outgoing, designing it so that it supports your intent, rather than sabotages it. You definitely want it to support your intent. Make sense?

We tend to get creative when we spend consciously, spending with intent and without debt. We can add all kinds of categories to the plan, like home improvement. We can also consider other ways of obtaining what we want—like partnering, collaborating, volunteering, swapping. You might choose to "attend" that concert or seminar by buying the tape rather than pay the costs of admittance and transportation. Choose wisely.

"Do I have to Use My Own Money?"

One of my sisters set an intent at an early age to avoid spending all her money. This is the same sister who managed to purchase three pieces of property while the rest of us were just beginning. When we were young, most Sundays we would go to church, have dinner, then go to the movies. My mother would check *Parents Magazine*, and if the movie was appropriate, off we would head to the movies, checking at the last minute to see if we all had our money with us. Invariably, this same sister would ask, "Do I have to use my own money?" If the answer was yes, she often changed her mind. "Then I'm not going." Of course we hated to see her miss out on the movies. We'd try to convince her to come along. Sometimes even paying her way. After all, what would she do at home by herself, anyhow? Now I think, "Probably count her money." But you see, since the rest of us didn't have any money, we couldn't imagine what somebody with some would do or think.

"Do I have to use my own money?" Because if I have to use my own money, I may think differently about the matter. We tend to treat our money as though it's Citibank's money or Visa's money. VISA doesn't have its own money. It has your money and it's your money they're investing. *You* want to decide about your money. You want to be more like my sister. "Oh, am I to use my money? Well, I may have to think about that. Let me look at my spending plan. Let me just consider this, because I've already restored my consciousness to its proper alignment. So when I discover that a purchase is going to require *my* money, I am fully prepared to make this decision from a place of empowerment. It is from an aligned consciousness in which I have already determined my priorities."

Being a good steward is not the same as being cheap. It is taking personal responsibility for handling and managing the divine flow of good in your life so that it keeps right on flowing, in every aspect of your life. Being a good steward means that you keep accurate records. You're recording all incoming, expected and unexpected. You're also recording all outgoing. If it's more than a dollar, you've got a record of it. How else can you know where you money is going if you haven't kept a record? And how can you know how best to use it without an intent to direct it? The record provides you the raw data—your own database, if you will. Just don't get attached to forms and special computer database software. Don't give yourself an excuse for not recording.

The data may also help you think differently about your money. You may catch things, important things, like overpayments, like excess. You may well decide that while digital cable is cute, basic cable is really enough—or maybe no cable at all. So goodbye, cable bill. And then you're free to re-direct the money you were spending for cable, to something that's more compatible with the clear higher intent you've set. Perhaps a vacation is more important, you know, extended fun. So you'll intentionally start paying for that cruise now. Vacationing is a lot more fun when you don't have to come back home and pay for it for a year—a whole lot more fun.

Be willing to hang out in a consciousness that continues to draw the opportunities to you. Be willing to break your old mold—remember, it is what got you into this financial state in the first place. This is the sacrifice. This is where you, in your inner knowingness, give up something of lesser value for the greater good. Remember to ask my sister's question: "Do I have to use my own money?"

Begin to free up your energy around money. Can you see that money is really trying to get to you? Have you set a clear intent regarding money? Are you preparing a space for it? If you don't have an investment account, why would investment money be coming to you? What would you do with that money that is intended for investing and broadening your financial universe? You're shifting and redirecting your energy in such a way that you can see that it's you who's blocking the flow, not your employer or union or family. Just as you stepped in to block the flow, you can step out of the way of the divine flow of good in your life. Praise God.

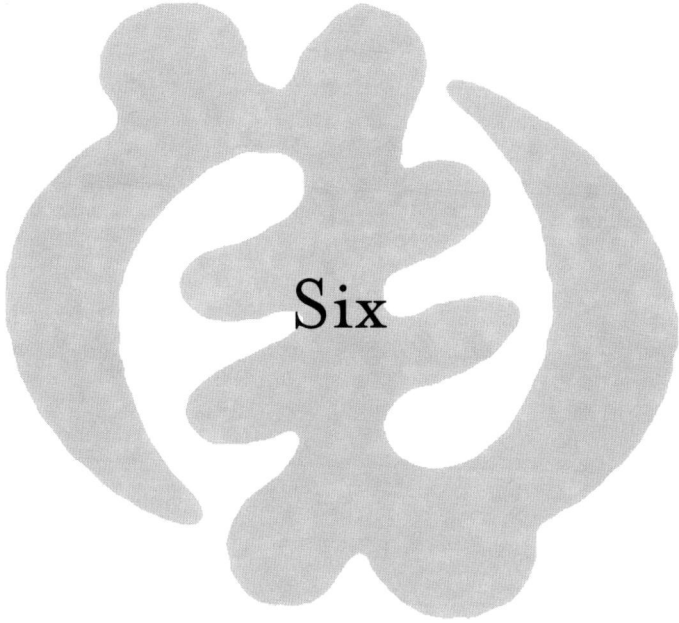

Six

*Do not conform any longer to the pattern of this world,
but be transformed by the renewing of your mind.*

Romans 12:2

SHIFTING YOUR PERCEPTION

What You See Is What You Get

I fertilize my mind with LOVE and increase
my receptivity to living a magnificent life.
I am open and available to infinite possibility.
I plant and harvest good, better, best.
I choose to experience my life as whole,
perfect and complete.

*M*y two nephews are my teachers. Russell is ten years old; his brother William is four, and he is practically my guru. As I study William interacting with, and allowing Divine Spirit to express as him, I am so inspired! "I can do that," I think. I am willing to "do as the spirit says do," as the old freedom song goes. I am willing not only to surrender the baggage that I drag along, but to revel in my surrender, to be as light as he is with God, in God, as God.

Recently my sister, the boys' mother, observed how often we tend to declare things we really don't want, how often we declare to the universe our own detriment in the same way we predict our good. She said the idea comes to her often as she watches her boys. It's the same declaring as when children declare that there's nothing to do, they're bored. Yes, I love to observe the children, because they make it so plain and simple. I can see it so clearly! I've actually seen the boys declare, "There's nothin' to eat" as they're standing in front of my refrigerator with the door open. They repeat, even louder, "I'm starvin' and there's nothing in here to eat!" as they move an item out of the way just to make sure there's nothing in there to eat.

There's an adult equivalent; "That job is mine. I will definitely have it. I don't care who else they interview. It's mine!" We declare this with the same mouth, same intellect, same knowingness and same power with which we decide, "He's leaving me! I know he doesn't love me." "I know she doesn't care about me and is just stringing me along. I know I'll not find my perfect partner because…(add any variety of damning reasons)." It is the same knowingness, the same energy, but we are directing it differently—to our own detriment.

What's the difference? Somebody please tell me. The only difference I see is age and terminology. And you'd think we're old enough to know better! Adults often declare in earnest, that there is no place for us where our good can be fully expressed. It's not unlike, as my sister reminded me, when we say we don't have anything to wear—you know, while we're standing in the closet, fully clothed, pushing nearly-new ensembles along the rod. We're still using the same energy (some might say misusing it). At any given moment, we're using that energy according to our willingness, our belief system, according to how we see ourselves.

As we talked, my sister shared an idea that she'd just read about and was planning to implement. (Watch this now, because it's something I believe that the child in us can utilize.) A parent took photographs of her children in a variety of activities—putting puzzles together, painting, playing outdoors—activities that really engaged them. Over the course of a few weeks she'd created a whole visual record of these little moments, records of the children in action. Whenever one or another child comes to declare (as they inevitably will—didn't we?) that there's nothing to do, whines that she's bored, the mother leads her to the board where she's already posted the photographs, ready for that predictable moment.

How wise, I think. Surely that applies to my life. Now, could that not work in my life? Could it not work when I say I'm unlovable? Could I not have had a plan in place where I have already collected some evidence of my being lovable? For surely there had to be a point in my life when I experienced being lovable. It might have been in the mirror, just with me. It may have been with somebody who allowed me to feel lovable for that moment. Lord yes! You see…Just for the moment… The details matter not.

I believe we would all do ourselves a favor by creating a similar reminder, a tangible record, of our most *centered* times, the times we feel most connected to the Divine. We can create one even if we don't take the time to take a stack of photographs. What is the best photography anyhow? The oldest camera? Requires no film? Has no need of digital technology? It's our magnificent mind! Isn't that how scientists came to understand the camera mechanism—by understanding how our ocular system operated? So, there's an opportunity for me to utilize this awesome mind of mine for my good. Perhaps I can capture a moment when I was hirable, or capture a moment when I was desirable. Perhaps I can capture a moment of absolute clarity of my divinity. Just a snapshot, a reminder. If I can capture just a moment of my connectedness with God... If just for a second, I can remember that prayer works when I speak my word...If just for a second, I can get that my word has power...If just for a millisecond I can get that *I am* and that is a good thing.

We don't have to "fake it to make it," as the saying goes. Life is always on our side, supporting our best self. We can choose to be fully present to the divine unfoldment of our lives. The key is to identify and mark our *center* (yes, similar to a dog's intent for marking its territory). Choose to recognize when you're there. Place your mental, emotional, physical and spiritual marks there as an identifiable stake to assist you in returning to this spot with increasing ease and grace over and over again, until this spot is transformed into the divine portal through which you transcend the demands and details of your life to settle in a place of wholeness, peace, serenity—a place that will expand the good in your life.

You might try to develop your sensory awareness to discern when you are authentically you, when you feel your best, when you do what you intend to do, when you say what matters from Truth, when you are happy with what you have...Develop your awareness in such a way that you are clear about you. In this state of consciousness you recognize and embrace your best self in all you do. You intentionally express yourself as you intended. You also discern what supported you in being there—specific thoughts, activities, beliefs, diet, focus, forgiving, loving, being peaceful, accepting.

As you "hit your mark", set an intent to establish a shortcut, a direct route to center, if you will. Be willing to engage whatever serves you: music, graphics, written and spoken words—whatever it is that when you hear it, see it, read it, sing it, feel it or *know* it, you experience being centered in the Truth about you and your connection to God.

To do so is to empower yourself. On some level, you already know what it takes for you to surrender your drama, to let it go and allow yourself to be your absolute best. Whatever else this requires, it must include setting an intent and focusing your attention on your intent to be and do your best. Especially in times of crisis, it serves you to think only the best, to provide yourself with a steady diet of good, better, best. (Remember, the ancient Chinese symbol for "crisis" combines the symbol connoting danger and the symbol connoting opportunity!) As you focus on your diet of better and best, you can also embrace the sacred *Yes* as a way to surrender into knowing—truly knowing—that the best is yet to come, and that it is being revealed through you. Whenever you do this, you strengthen your spiritual muscle, expand your awareness, and fuel your resolve to allow yourself to be gracefully guided out of the abyss, out of this dark night of your soul. Whenever you let go of appearance, you open the portal of infinite possibility.

We Can All Use An Empowerment Binder

Similar to capturing the truth through photographs taken for our children, we can begin to capture and assemble the objects and ideas that help to launch our spirit and remind us visually of where we want to be emotionally and spiritually—how we want to be and see ourselves. My own "gimmick" is my *Personal Success Empowerment Binder*. I created one for myself several years ago, and I assign this project to some of my clients. I use mine regularly. It's my "transformation bible" of sorts, an inspiring image book filled to the brim with my personal collection of favorite affirmations, prayers, quotations, pictures, stories, poems, etc. Its contents contain essentially anything that, when I see it or read it, supports me in embracing the Truth about me, my life, my circumstances and the infinite possibilities available to me. Any page or line in my binder serves to empower me and launch my spirits. I use it like a prescription—I use it when I anticipate an ache, and I definitely use it to relieve the aches and pains of daily life. Life has taught me that pain is inevitable, but there is much I can do to alleviate suffering. My binder helps me minimize the pain and eliminate the suffering. I invite you to join me in creating and applying such a potent tool.

You might begin your own *Your Personal Success Empowerment Binder* by writing down your favorite affirmations, quotations and lyrics. Whenever you see or hear something that has a positive effect on your mental, emotional or spiritual state, capture it and add it to your binder. Be sure to include pictures (you know, they're worth a thousand words). I have photos of vibrant Hawaiian flowers and travel scenes, both of which help me get centered.

So go for it! The intent is to insert several consciousness items into an empowerment binder of your own. The litmus test: Can you open it, allow your eyes to fall on any single item, and begin a discernable shift of consciousness that launches your spirit in the direction you intend? If so, keep it up. Use it daily. Let it support your shift toward embracing the whole you.

Remember: Only the best thoughts for you. You're worth it!

Epilogue

*I*magine that right where you are, in this exact moment, a switch is flipped and your life is flooded with light. The light is so bright that you now see all the roads you traveled to this moment. Everything that ever happened in your life is revealed. You see how every breath you breathed is linked with another and gave birth to this very breath. In this bright light you can clearly recognize your center. You are looking at the spiritual path through your life.

Our goal is to get back to center. Wish we had dropped breadcrumbs on the way out, huh? I sure wish I had, and I make certain I leave a trail now. But, since I did not start out leaving myself a trail of breadcrumbs, a way of tracking my way back to center, I have had to design a map for myself. The themes, words and affirmations in this book have essentially served as my map to guide me home, and I am honored to have shared them with you. I pray that this book has illuminated the infinite possibilities already available in your life, and inspired you to celebrate yourself, embrace your wholeness and live in spiritual congruence.

So let the good times begin....

Let's celebrate!
Andriette

Here's how you can work with Andriette:

Andriette presents enlightening workshops on a variety of success topics. She is also available to custom-design and present workshops for groups and organizations with specific success goals in mind. Andriette has conducted an impressive array of workshops, retreats and speaking engagements in the United States, Europe, South America and Mexico. Her approach emphasizes personal mastery and self-surrender as key transformational tools. She is committed to revealing divine order behind and within every experience as a substantial and tremendously valuable investment in life.

Your Personal Success offers "Destiny by Design" in:
  Dynamic Motivational Presentations
  Inspirational Success Workshops, Sessions and Retreats
  Interactive Audio-cassette Series ("Workshops-to-go")
  Self-Empowerment Tools
  Compassionate Spiritual Counseling
  Transformational Life/Success Coaching

You can arrange to bring *Your Personal Success* sessions to your area. Visit the author's Web site at www.yourpersonalsuccess.com to request her as a speaker, workshop/retreat facilitator or success coach. Please also visit the online Success Store, where you'll find further information on her audio tapes and other empowerment tools.

To invite Andriette and determine how she can best contribute to the success of your next event, email or mail your contact information, inquiry and comments to Your Personal Success, 484 Lake Park Avenue #220, Oakland, CA 94610.

Make a Commitment to Your Personal Success Today!

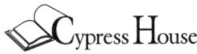

Cypress House

Order Form

Embracing Wholeness: Living in Spiritual Congruence

by Andriette Earl-Bozeman

	Number of books ordered @ $15.00 each	SUBTOTAL ☞	
☐	Please put me on your book catalog mailing list.	7.25% sales tax (CA residents only)	
	Shipping & handling charges: $3.00 USPS or $5.00 UPS or priority mail, plus $1.00 for each additional book.	Shipping & handling ☞	
	Name	**Total** ☞	

Address	Ship to
City / State / Zip	Address
☐ Check enclosed / *Charge to:* ☐ VISA ☐ MasterCard	City / State / Zip

Card Number	Expiration Date
Authorized Cardholder Signature	Daytime Phone Number

Send your order to: Cypress House
155 Cypress Street · Fort Bragg, CA 95437
or call **1-800-773-7782**
You can also fax your credit card order to 707-964-7531
or visit our website at www.cypresshouse.com